FORTY DAYS OF TRANSFORMATION

Daily Reflections of Teshuvah for Spiritual Growth
From Rosh Hodesh Elul to Yom Kippur

DOV PERETZ ELKINS

GROWTH ASSOCIATES
Princeton, NJ

ISBN 0-918834-20-1
Library of Congress Catalog Card Number: 99-63180

Printed in the United States of America

For a complete catalog of books contact:

Growth Associates Publishers
212 Stuart Road East
Princeton, NJ 08540-1946
609/497-7375
E-mail: elkins@tigger.jvnc.net
Web Site: www.DPElkins.com

To my friends and students at
The Jewish Center of Princeton, NJ

"From my teachers I have learned much,

from my colleagues even more,

from my students, the most."

Talmud, Ta-anit 7

ACKNOWLEDGMENTS

No parts of this collection may be reprinted or reproduced in any media without written permission from the copyright holder. All attempts have been made to obtain permission from holders of copyrights from authors and publications included. Any oversight in this regard will be corrected should a second printing be warranted, and apologies are offered to anyone regarding any possible errors. Please communicate any matters relating to this subject to the editor at the address on the title page.

Grateful acknowledgment is offered to those rabbis, authors, editors and publishers, who graciously granted permission to use their material for this collection. These include Rabbis Danny Horwitz, Eric M. Lankin, Stephen Weiss, Lawrence Kushner, Sanford Ragins, Stephen Chaim Listfield, Bernard S. Raskas, Harold Schulweis, Samuel B. Press, Maurice Davis z"l, Joseph Braver z"l, Rami Shapiro, Steven Carr Reuben.

To Heal The Soul: The Spiritual Journal of a Chasidic Rebbe, by Rabbi Kalonymus Kalman Shapira, trans. Yehoshua Starrett, 1995, pp. 123-4, reprinted by permission of the publisher, Jason Aronson, Inc., Northvale, NJ © 1995; Rabbi Yehuda Appel of Aish HaTorah of Cleveland, OH; Mesorah Publications for *A Treasury of Chassidic Tales on the Festivals*, by Rabbi S.Y.Zevin, p. 70; Monique Pasternak and *Four Winds Journal* (Vol. III, #3); Prof. Arthur Green for selection from *Restoring the Aleph: Judaism for the Contemporary Seeker* (NY: Council for Initiatives in Jewish Education, 1996, pp. 14-15); Beth Huppin; Rabbi David Hartman from *Conflicting Visions: Spiritual Possibilities for Israel* (Schocken, 1990); Burning Bush Press of the United Synagogue for Conservative Judaism; Prof. Deborah E. Lipstadt from *The Jewish Spectator*, Fall, 1993; Gustine Matt for material from *Walking Humbly With God* by Rabbi Hershel Matt (KTAV, 1993); Crown Publishers for material from Rabbi Morris Adler, *May I Have A Word With You?*.

THE CENTRALITY OF TESHUVAH

My understanding of the concept of Teshuvah has been powerfully influenced by the writings of Rabbi Avraham Yitzhak Kook, first Chief Rabbi of Eretz Yisrael (d. 1935). My late teacher, Rabbi Ben Zion Bokser, in the introduction to his translation of Rav Kook's seminal and popular book, *Orot HaTeshuvah - The Lights of Penitence* (in *Abraham Isaac Kook*, Paulist Press, 1978, p. 39) writes about Kook's radical definition of Teshuvah in these words:

"The conventional conception of penitence sees it as an effort to redress a particular transgression in the area of man's relationship to God or to his fellowman. For Rabbi Kook penitence is the surge of the soul for perfection, to rise above the limitations imposed by the finitude of existence. It is a reach for reunion with God.... Penitence in man is, in other words, only one episode in the entire drama of cosmic life, which is forever seeking higher levels of development.... Its primary focus is the quest for self-perfection, but it overflows into the endeavor to perfect society and the world."

In an important note, Rabbi Bokser goes further in his exploration of Rav Kook's notion of Teshuvah. "Kook believed that an evil deed is an impulse that at its highest source of origin was good but became distorted and went astray. The righteous judge everything from the perspective of its highest motivation and therefore including everything in the good."

This radical notion of Teshuvah is so vastly different from the common notion of "repentance," which has such heavy theological overtones of sin, that it makes one wonder if there truly is an English word which accurately translates the Hebrew "Teshuvah." *Transformation* is the closest I could come, and thus chose that word for the title of this spiritual anthology.

The goal of the book is to help people become better, rather than to have them emerge from the pits of guilt and self-flagellation. This is at heart a Hasidic idea, which Rav Kook borrowed and embellished. It is also a humanistic idea which is so much more understandable to the modern mind, attuned to the writings of Abraham Maslow, Carl Rogers, Rollo May, and other modern teachers of the spirit. At heart, it is the Jewish idea that humans are made in the image of God - an optimistic view of life, humanity, and spiritual possibilities.

Readers should use this text as a cook book, taking from it what they will, bits at a time, and mixing it with their own personal ingredients, so that the ultimate creation is unique and different from the prescription of a printed text.

I am grateful to Almighty God for the privilege of assembling these readings in the hope that the exquisite period in the Jewish calendar most appropriate for spiritual growth will be one that leads each individual, his/her family, society, and beyond, to a better world.

Dov Peretz Elkins
Princeton, NJ
Yom Ha-Atzmaut, 5759

FORTY DAYS OF TRANSFORMATION

Daily Reflections of Teshuvah for Spiritual Growth
From Rosh Hodesh Elul to Yom Kippur

DOV PERETZ ELKINS

1 Rosh Hodesh Elul

CLEANSED WITH TEARS

Reb Elimelech and Reb Zusya had a third brother - a village tavernkeeper. Now would it not be interesting to find out what manner of man this was? Surely he was no common fellow! Fired by curiosity, the disciples of Reb Elimelech decided one day to make the journey to his village, in order to find out for themselves. There, sure enough, they found him - standing foursquare behind the counter of his tavern, selling vodka to the surly yokels of the province. There was certainly no hint here of any spiritual flights to the lofty Worlds Above. All they noticed was that from time to time he took out his little notebook and wrote a few words in it.

The bar was closed at nightfall and they asked to sleep in the inn. Then, late at night, when the household was fast asleep, they listened in from the room adjoining his, and heard him turning pages and reading to himself, from time to time striking himself on the chest and weeping bitterly all the while.

Overcome by inquisitiveness they walked right into his room and asked- "How is it that a man should *strike* himself?"

Their host answered them simply that this was his regular custom. Every day, whenever it seemed to him that he had sinned in some way, or that an unholy thought had crossed his mind, he noted this in his little notebook. Then, when night came, he would never go to sleep until he had repented with a *teshuva* that came from the bottom of his heart. And he even had a sign by which he could know whether his repentance had been found acceptable in the eyes of Heaven. For when he saw that the ink in his notebook was blotted out by his tears, then he knew that in Heaven too his sins had been erased.

Rabbi S. Y. Zevin
A Treasury of Chassidic Tales on the Festivals
(NY.- Artscroll Mesorah Series, p. 70)

TO DISCUSS:

Are tears required to truly repent?

What signs can you use to know that your repentance is sincere?

TO DO:

Today I will judge people by their actions, not by appearances.

2 Elul

JOINING IN THE GREAT RETURN

Teshuvah is the ever-present possibility, urge and gesture of returning to our Source, the Holy One of All Being. Through teshuvah all life is returned to its source. As Rav Kook teaches, it flows unnoticed throughout creation. Teshuvah is not simply apologizing or making right the damage we have done, though these are prerequisites. It is only this: The Return. *Teshuvah* is the hardest thing in the world, for to fully make it would bring the Messiah. But it is also the easiest thing, since the process of teshuvah begins with the simple thought of wanting to begin.

More than just an individual gesture, teshuvah is a great world-yearning that flows through and animates all creation. Through attempting to repair and heal what we have done in the past, we set it within a larger context of meaning and effectively rewrite the past. What was once only some thoughtless or even wicked act, now - when viewed from the perspective of our present *teshuvah* - becomes only the embarrassing commencement of this greater healing now realized.

We stubbornly and despite all the evidence look forward to a time when all creation will join in the Great Return - a unity of all the world reflecting the Unitary Source of all Creation.

Rabbi Lawrence Kushner, *Moment Magazine*, December, 1992, pp. 45-46

4

TO DISCUSS:

How does teshuvah flow "unnoticed throughout creation?" Why is teshuvah both the hardest and the easiest thing in the world?

How can the author portray a wicked act as the beginning of a great healing?

TO DO:

Today I will find a way to join all creation in the Great Return, reflecting the Unitary Source of all creation.

3 Elul

TESHUVAH

Like ripe fruits
our lives have fallen back to earth
to release their seeds on the spiral of time.
As we lie awake in the dark tunnels of turning,
the electric nights of Elul tear
at our flesh; in the morning
the sound of the shofar
    -our sole link to memory-
breaks the air and calls the soul.
For 40 days and 40 nights
we waver, suspended, until
naked in its promise the seed stands
and the spark of judgment returns
to ignite our life.

© Monique Pasternak, *Flying On The Wings of Aleph*

6

TO DISCUSS:

How does the spark of judgment ignite our life?

How do the nights of Elul tear at our flesh?

Where is the note of optimism in the poem?

TO DO:

Today I will hear the sound of the Shofar calling my soul to ignite my life.

4 Elul

SHAPING THE IMAGE OF THE COMING YEAR

My friend, Kansas City Jewish community leader Merilyn Berenbom, tells this story from her childhood.

My father was a lawyer, and he happened to have as one of his clients the well-known artist Thomas Hart Benton. Occasionally, when I was a young child, our family would visit at his house, where he had a large studio, with a broad wall where he would create his famous murals. And with every mural, even while the wall was still blank, the studio would have in it sculptures and paintings. For before creating any character in the mural itself, Benton would make an entire sculpture of that individual, and do paintings of that character, so as to effectively capture what it was that he wanted to create.

And so I have reflected since then about how important it is to capture a vision of what we want to create, before we go about building it.

And as we approach the beginning of the New Year, we reflect about why we are here. Through our prayers, through reflection, through sincere teshuvah...we are doing the work of shaping the bust, the image, of the year we seek to create. It remains for us to make the final "mural" of our lives by shaping our characters, day to day, throughout the rest of the year.

Rabbi Daniel M. Horwitz

TO DISCUSS:

What vision do you have of your future?

TO DO:

Make a drawing - or a painting, or a sculpture - of what you want your life to look like.

5 Elul

BAAL TESHUVAH: HOLY OF HOLIES

"This is the Torah [teaching] of the guilt offering:
it is holy of holies."

Leviticus 7:1

The question raised by the commentators on this verse is why the sacrifice of one who has sinned is termed "holy of holies." That special, high category should be reserved for one who has never sinned. Not so, says the *Kli Yakar*, Rabbi Shlomo Ephraim Lunshitz (1550 - 1619, Lemberg and Prague), who explains that a perfect tzaddik (wise, enlightened one) is called "holy," while a person who sins and brings an offering (i.e., who repents) is called "holy of holies."

This is in accord with the Talmud that states (Sanhedrin 99a): "A very saintly person cannot compare with the high level of those who have sinned and repented."

For proof of this, the *Kli Yakar* quotes another talmudic passage (Yoma 86a) that teaches that the wicked acts of a repentant person are transformed into merits! Thus, one who sins and repents receives credit for good deeds as well as for sins, which are now considered as merits. A tzaddik only has good deeds, and is , holy; but a repentant sinner has good deeds *and* merits for repentance, and is "holy of holies."

Rabbi Dov Peretz Elkins
(from *Sidrah Sparks*, Parashat Tzav)

TO DISCUSS:

Do you agree that a repentant sinner is more worthy than one who never sinned?

What if one sins in order to repent and become higher than one who never sinned?

TO DO:

Today I will transform my mistakes into merits.

6 Elul

THE BINDING OF YITZHAK
AND THE BINDING OF YOU AND ME

The month of Elul is a good time to think about some of life's important lessons. The Forty Days of Transformation, during Elul and the Ten Days of Repentance, are a time to evaluate our relationship with important people in our lives. We ask their forgiveness, they ask ours, and if there is regret for past faults and insensitive acts (Tradition calls them "sins"), we lend forgiveness to others, and they to us.

Now is also a time to think about our relation with our Tradition, with Judaism. It will soon be the Jewish New Year, a time to reexamine where are stand with regard to the faith/culture/civilization we call Judaism..

Take a few moments - or a few hours - to think about and discuss your Jewish values and priorities with your loved ones and intellectual dialog partners. How can you deepen and strengthen your Jewish ties and commitments in the coming year?

Perhaps that is why we are bidden to hear the sound of the Shofar each morning during the month of Elul. The Talmud, in tractate "Rosh Hashanah" (16a), tells us: "Rabbi Abahu said: Why do we use the horn of a *ram* on Rosh Hashanah? Because the Blessed Holy One is saying to us: If you blow a horn from a ram before Me on Rosh Hashanah, I will be reminded of the act of ultimate faith performed by Avraham when he was ready to carry out my demand, even though a ram was eventually sacrificed in place of Yitzhak. The merit of Avraham will reflect merit on you, his descendants. In fact, when you blow the Shofar, and I remember the Binding (Hebrew: *Akedah*) of Yitzhak I will attribute to you the merit of having bound (Hebrew: *akad-tem*) yourselves to me.

As we begin to blow the Shofar each morning, from the first day of the month of Elul, let's begin to think about how we bind ourselves to God. About our Jewish boundaries, the ties that bind us to our Jewish past. Let's think of how our ritual lives can be enriched and enhanced with more song, custom, prayer and ceremony. Let's think of how we can share ourselves with more Jewish causes (Israel, Jewish education, the synagogue), and how being Jewish can help bind and tie us to the needs of humanity (the environment, our community, the eradication of poverty and injustice).

Rabbi Dov Peretz Elkins

TO DISCUSS:

How does the ram sacrificed instead of Yitzhak help us remember to be more faithful Jews?

In what way can the story of the "Binding of Yitzhak" help to bind us to our people and our Creator?

TO DO:

Today I will find new ways to bind myself to the history of our People.

7 Elul

DO WE REALLY WANT TO CHANGE?

A woman proudly hung on her mantelpiece a needlework plaque that said "Prayer Changes Things." A few days later, the plaque was missing from its place. The woman asked her husband if he had seen it. "I took it down, I didn't like it," her husband replied.

"But why?" the woman asked. "Don't you believe that prayer changes things?" "Yes, I honestly do," her husband answered. "But it just so happens that I don't like change, so I threw it away."

None of us likes change. Yes, we will mouth many prayers during the holy days. But few of us really intend that these prayers will either begin a process of change or reflect a changing lifestyle. Some of us are happy with our lives and see no reason to change. Others of us, who are unhappy with our lives, may not have the necessary courage to make the changes needed to orient our goals with the goals of the Holy One.

But we live in a time where many are disconnected to the source of enduring values. Values that we assumed were societal standards have been tossed aside. During this High Holy Day season, we need to muster the courage to face our lives honestly and to overcome our fear of the unknown. We need to reconnect ourselves to the moorings of Jewish tradition and return to a life informed by God's teachings. When we do offer the words of the ancient prayers, let those prayers help us return to God, challenge us to resolve to be better, and help us not fall into the trap of repeating the mistakes that we have made.   Rabbi Eric M. Lankin

TO DISCUSS:

Do you believe that prayer changes things?

Do you really want to change?   What do you want to change?

TO DO:

Today I will begin a process to change something important in my life.

8 Elul

ARE WE HARDER THAN STONE?

Of my favorite places in Israel is Rosh Hanikrah. These magnificent grottos, on the northernmost coast of Israel, were carved out of limestone by the pounding of waves over thousands of years. The intricate lace of caves and tunnels goes deep into the rock, and is graced on the outside by dramatic cliffs and unusual rock formations shaped by the water. Michelangelo used to say that he did not create his sculptures. They were hidden within his stone. He simply revealed them. In the same way, it always seemed to me that the beauty of Rosh Hanikrah's grottos must have been hidden within the rock by God, waiting to be revealed by the water.

It is hard to imagine how something as soft as water can have such a transforming effect on something as hard as stone. Visiting there this summer, with the a Teen Mission, I was reminded again of that famous story of Rabbi Akiva. At the age of 40, Akiva had not studied a word of Torah. A shepherd by trade, no doubt he was intimidated by the rabbis of the academy. How could a country boy such as he ever master the sacred text? Then one day Akiva was standing by the mouth of a well. He noticed that the water dripped out; and his gaze followed the drip to a bowl shaped stone. He wondered aloud: "Who hollowed out this stone?" "Akiva," he was told, "haven't you read [in the book of Job] that 'water wears away stone?' It is the constant drip of the water, day after day, which created the hollow in the rock."

At that moment Akiva came to a realization. "Is my mind harder than stone?" he asked himself. "I will go and study at least one section of Torah.!" He went directly to the schoolhouse, where he began to read with his son. First the teacher wrote an alef and a bet, and he learned to read them. Like the dripping water, he worked his way through the entire Hebrew alphabet, letter by letter. Then he learned the book of Leviticus, and finally the entire Torah and the Oral Law. In the end, Akiva became one of the greatest sages there has ever been.

The story of Rabbi Akiva's beginning contains a great truth about life. Our most significant accomplishments do not come about in one grand moment. They are earned gradually, over time, little by little. If we were to try to accomplish our goals in one fell swoop, we would give up, thinking the task impossible.

Transformation requires patient determination. What we need most is to be like Rabbi Akiva. To look at the well of Torah and ask ourselves, "Am I harder than stone?" Drip by drip, day by day, challenge by challenge, we can make ourselves over again, if we try. And as we change, like the grottos of Rosh Hanikrah, the beauty that lies hidden within becomes revealed.   Rabbi Stephen Weiss

TO DISCUSS:

What significant accomplishments in the world took many years and did not occur in "one grand moment?"

What are the difficulties in being a "long distance runner," as opposed to a "sprint" achiever?

TO DO:

Today I will find an area of myself that is hidden in the stone that is my body and my being., and let it find a voice.

Today I will conceive of a project to enrich my spirit over a period of many years.

9 Elul

DEDICATE YOUR LIFE TO SPIRITUAL PROGRESS

[Rabbi Kalonymus Kalman Shapira died in Treblinka in 1943, after being a rabbi in the Warsaw Ghetto. He became a pioneer in journal-writing, and recommends this method of personal & spiritual growth in his diary. His teachings have been re-discovered and translated in recent years, and he is becoming known as one of the great spiritual teachers of our day].

If you have been able to compile relevant maxims and personal rules for your spiritual growth, wonderful! But if not, it shows that you have not devoted yourself and your life to growing, or, that you are some sort of being without a personal identity.

Because whoever dedicates his life to spiritual progress will inevitably be confronted by difficulties and impediments. These will not only be external, such as making a livelihood, but also internal blocks: indolence, negative tendencies, destructive character traits, and so forth. Someone who is constantly involved in the inner struggle for self-improvement sometimes wins and sometimes loses. From experience, conclusions can be drawn: when you do this, You win; when you do that, you lose.

Since no two people are alike in character and tendencies, and the inner struggles, successes, and failures of each are not the same, each person must draw up his own guidelines and self-advice, which will be different from any other's, each tailored for his own unique inner experience. So if one has not come up with his own guidebook to the spiritual life, it is either because he has not dedicated his life to struggling for self-improvement (in which case he knows of neither loss nor gain) or he is some anonymous being, so unaware of his own self that he cannot identify his unique inner struggle - the purpose of his being.

To Heal The Soul: The Spiritual Journal of a Chasidic Rebbe, Rabbi Kalonymus Kalman Shapira, trans. Yehoshua Starrett (Jason Aronson, 1995, pp. 123-4)

TO DISCUSS:

What maxims and personal rules have ever helped you?

What is your personal unique inner struggle?

TO DO:

Today I will seriously consider keeping a personal journal of my own progress in spiritual growth.

10 Elul

TESHUVAH ACCORDING TO THE TORAH: "RETURN" - NOT "REPENTANCE"

....Various sources discuss the importance of asking forgiveness from others before Yom Kippur. Jewish tradition points out that it does little good to ask forgiveness from G-d when one has harmed one's fellow. Because it is not G-d Who must extend forgiveness; rather, forgiveness must come from the individual who has been wronged!

According to many commentaries, the Biblical source for the mitzvah of Teshuva is found in the Torah portion of Nitzavim. The Torah instructs someone who has transgressed to "return to the L-rd your G-d." This understanding of Teshuva as a process of "return" is embedded in the word itself which (though commonly mistranslated as "repentance") actually means "return." Teshuva is the process by which we reestablish our connection to the Almighty and return to the basic goodness that is human nature.

Judaism, being a religion of action, says it is not enough to "mentally" regret one's misdeeds. On this verse that "very close is this (matter of Teshuva) to your mouth," Nachmanides takes this passage literally; he understands that Teshuva requires verbal articulation of our misdeeds.

In instances where someone else was wronged, an apology must be made directly to that person. In instances where we transgressed the Almighty's will, we must privately, with no one listening, confess to our Creator.

Rabbi Yehuda Appel
Aish HaTorah, Cleveland

TO DISCUSS:

Why is a distinction made between "repent" and "return?"

Do you agree that it is necessary to ask forgiveness from the person offended before God can forgive you?

TO DO:

Today I will return to the basic goodness in my human nature.

11 Elul

"THERE IS A MEANING BEYOND ABSURDITY"

In the famous interview that Carl Stern of NBC had with the late Rabbi Abraham Joshua Heschel, three weeks before Heschel's untimely death in 1972, Stern asked the famous rabbi: "What message have you for young people?"

Rabbi Heschel replied: "Let them remember that there is a meaning beyond absurdity. Let them be sure that every deed counts, that every word has power, and that we all can do our share to redeem the world in spite of all absurdities and all frustrations and all disappointments.... And above all, let them remember... to build a life as if it were a work of art."

TO DISCUSS:

How can you do your share to redeem the world?

TO DO:

Today I will endeavor to build my life as if it were a work of art.

12 Elul

HUMANITY IS INDIVISIBLE

How does the Jewish mind work? We learned that from Teddy Kollek, the [former] Mayor of Jerusalem, when he was awarded the annual Peace Prize of the Association of German Publishers recently. The ceremony took place in the historic Paulskirche in Frankfurt. When Kollek was asked to designate someone to present the award, he made a surprising choice. He picked Manfred Rommel, now the mayor of Stuttgart, and the son of General Erwin Rommel.

After receiving the prize, Kollek responded. He explained that he had chosen Rommel to make the presentation because he remembered the battle of El Alamein and the "great danger that the German army, under Field Marshall Rommel, posed in [that] part of the world. The fate of the Jewish people of Palestine [now Israel] seemed mortally threatened."

"Who would have imagined then, [Kollek asked] that the Field Marshall's son and I would meet in the peaceful profession of being Mayors? Isn't that a symbol of peace, which is our theme here?" And then Kollek added these remarkable words:

"In the face of the fanaticism and intolerance which are the mark of our times, there is a need for a deep belief in humanistic Jewishness ... treating all [people] with the same respect and in the same manner. That isn't always recognized, especially among groups which only think of themselves and overlook the interests of others.... According to Jewish belief, [however] humanity is indivisible."

Rabbi Sanford Ragins, from *The American Rabbi*, August, 1994

TO DISCUSS:

What did Mayor Teddy Kollek mean by "humanistic Jewishness?"

In what way will the idea of an indivisible humanity help change the world?

TO DO:

Today I will treat all people with the same respect and in the same manner.

13 Elul

TESHUVAH FOR LUTHER'S ANTI-SEMITISM

Dianna Dunken Rowe is a direct descendent of Martin Luther. She lives in the small town of Sylacauga, Alabama, outside of Birmingham. In September, 1997, when she found out about all the terrible things Martin Luther said about the Jews, and how his influence helped cause Hitler to carry out his nefarious acts, she bowed down and prayed to God how to expiate her sense of guilt. Her answer was to send out a postcard to 4000 synagogues throughout America.

A colleague of mine called her to tell her she need not apologize to him, because he didn't suffer from anti-Semitism, but that her act was a noble deed which falls into the Jewish rubric of "Teshuvah", causing regret and forgiveness. She cried on the phone and ask the rabbi to read her message to his congregation. She is obviously a saintly woman who is trying to do a bit of good in our world filled with hate, bitterness and discrimination. Here is her postcard, quoted in full:

Dear Rabbi and Jewish Congregation,

I am a DESCENDANT OF MARTIN LUTHER, who wrote many anti-Semitic tracts during the 16th century. I hang my head in shame and I have great sorrow in my heart for the tracts he wrote and for the influence that his writings had on those who persecuted the Jewish people...especially Hitler. Hitler used Luther's tracts to justify the atrocities that he directed towards the chosen people of God! The deep wounds of the holocaust remain fresh today in the

26

hearts of many and only the love and mercy of God can bring about healing; however, I OFFER MY SINCERE APOLOGY TO YOU for the pain that resulted from Luther's writings. I have gone before the Lord in intercessory REPENTANCE FOR THE SINS OF MY FAMILY AND I ALSO ASK FOR YOUR FORGIVENESS!

As you prepare to enter into Rosh Hashanah and Yom Kippur, I pray that you will open your hearts to FORGIVE MY FAMILY. I thank you for your willingness to read this note of apology and I pray that God's gift of healing and restoration will be yours this year. Just as the Book of Ruth tells the story of the special love that the Lord placed in the heart of the gentile woman towards the Jewish people and the special love that they returned to her, I pray that this note will initiate the same healing and restoration.
Shalom,
Dianna Dunken Rowe
Post Office Box 663
Sylacauga, Alabama 35150

TO DISCUSS:
Do you think it was necessary for Ms. Rowe to offer an apology to the Jewish people?

How would you answer her letter?

TO DO:
Today I will offer an apology to someone who needs it, even if they think I am not required to do so.

14 Elul

TESHUVAH AS ENDING SELF-EXILE

There are three types of exile and they are of increasing severity. The first is when Jews are in exile among other nations.

The second is when Jews are in exile among other Jews.

The third and most severe is when a Jew is alien to him/herself, for then s/he is both captor and captive, in exile within him/herself.

Rabbi Sholom ben Elazar Rokeah of Belz
(1779-1855)

TO DISCUSS:

Why is being alienated from oneself the worst kind of exile?

TO DO:

Today I will strive to bring myself back to my true nature, and keep myself close to my own soul.

15 Elul

OUR ACTIONS AFFECT OUR
CHILDREN'S HUMANITY -
AND OUR CHILDREN AFFECT THE WORLD

An experience in the life of Bishop Desmond Tutu, Nobel Peace Laureate and Episcopal Archbishop of South Africa, had a profound affect on his later life. When asked to name a childhood experience that empowered him to work for social justice, he recalled an incident in which, as a youngster, he saw a white man tip his hat to a black woman.

The woman, noted Tutu, was my mother, and the man was an Episcopal bishop!

TO DISCUSS:

Think of an act that influenced you for good when you were younger?

TO DO:

Today I will behave in ways that may affect the younger generation.

16 Elul

HASIDISM IS ABOUT THIS: *Arbetn oif zikh* - "TO WORK ON YOURSELF"

A number of years ago my family and I were living in Berkeley, CA. Around the corner from us was, of course, a spiritual or New Age bookstore. The front of the store was decorated with a huge sign, in inverted pyramid form. The top line read, in large block letters: SCIENTOLOGY DOESN'T WORK. Beneath that, in slightly smaller letters, it said: INTEGRAL YOGA DOESN'T WORK. Then, again slightly smaller: CHRISTIANITY DOESN'T WORK. After going through six or seven more would-be spiritual paths the sign concluded, again in large letters: YOU WORK. Seeing this sign reminded me of a definition of Hasidism that Abraham Joshua Heschel had passed on in the name of the Kotsker rebbe. When asked what Hasidism was all about, Rabbi Mendel of Kotsk replied: "*Arbetn oif zikh*" - "**to work on yourself.**"

Rabbi Arthur Green, Philip W. Lown Professor of Jewish Thought, Brandeis University
Restoring The Aleph - Judaism For The Contemporary Seeker (NY: Council for Initiatives in Jewish Education,1996, pp. 14-15)

TO DISCUSS:

Why is the difference between making scientology or yoga work, and making "you" work?

What point is the sign trying to make?

TO DO:

Today I will take seriously the Hasidic approach to Teshuvah, and I will work on myself.

17 Elul

JUDGING OTHERS AND YOURSELF

A person can check his/her own spiritual health and status in the following way: If your manner of judging others is to presume that they are worthy and to see their value, then you are surely a person of holiness and spiritual health.

On the other hand, if you tend to judge people negatively, to see their faults and to speak critically of them, then you had better realize that you are spiritually sick. You need to consult your rabbi right away.

In this regard our Sages taught, "Who is wise? — A person who learns from everyone" (Avot 4:1). Midrashically, we interpret this to mean that a wise person learns from **her/himself**. That is, he/she recognizes and admits his/her faults. This person is humble and modest. This is the opposite of the kind of person who is so good at criticizing others, yet is blissfully unaware of his own faults.

This same idea is found in the Zohar, Parshat Pekude: The palace of holiness contains a special room called "merit," while the den of nastiness has a room called "guilt" (we might call it a "hall of shame"). The difference between the two is simply this: The souls who go to a place of merit are the kind of people who see the good in others. It follows, therefore, that God sees the good in them. He assigns them to the place of holiness and merit. Even those who might not be the most all-around wonderful people — if they see the good in others, God judges them for good. Conversely, the "hall of shame" is filled with people who shame, criticize and speak ill of other people. And it's important to remember that this is the way that every person can gauge his own spiritual health, and know exactly where his soul is headed. You look for good in others — God looks for good in you. You look for bad, so does God....

(Translated by Rabbi Stephen Chaim Listfield, from *Perakim Bemahshevet Hahasidut*)

TO DISCUSS:

Why do most people judge others harshly and themselves gently? How can we change this, in accordance with the advice of the sages quoted above?

TO DO:

Today I will look for only the good in others, and search for my own faults.

18 Elul

A LESSON FROM KING HUSSEIN

[When 7 Israeli youth were killed by a crazed Jordanian soldier in March, 1997, an American visiting Israel with her family wrote this note:]

This was the evening that it happened and grief was overwhelming. The girls were buried that very night. The next morning the girls' pictures covered the front page of the paper. And, again, the stories. I couldn't bear to watch TV or read the stories at first. It was just too much. One of the girls, it turns out, was the translator for her parents who are deaf and unable to speak. She was their link to the world. There is no end to these stories. I felt overwhelmed. How do people live here year in and year out with tragedies like this? The words of the woman in the store came back to me. We have nowhere else to go.

But then, in the midst of our grief, King Hussein came. It was the most remarkable thing I have ever seen. All of Israel was glued to the television. His humility, his sincerity, his ability to say "I'm sorry" was a true gift to this county. To see this King, on his KNEES, in the homes of these Jewish families—listening, comforting, apologizing on behalf of his people—it was absolutely unbelievable. The whole country was in tears watching this. And he really did comfort this country in a way that nobody could have imagined possible. He won the hearts of this country. He had the courage to say "I'm sorry". Who was the last politician you've seen who has said, "I'm sorry". He could have easily discounted this crazy soldier as unstable and unrepresentative of the Jordanian army. He would have had every grounds to do that. Isn't that what we said about Baruch Goldstein, when he began shooting in Hebron?

[Editor's footnote: King Hussein kept contact with the family he visited even during his final illness. After King Hussein's death in 1999, the family whom he visited during Shiva had another child, and named her Jordana. They wanted to keep the King's act of compassion alive].

Beth Huppin

TO DISCUSS:

Why is the impact of a compassionate act by a well-known leader so powerful on the world's psyche?

TO DO:

Today I will make a special effort to reach out to someone of a different group than mine.

19 Elul

TESHUVAH: ISRAEL AND PALESTINIANS

Rabbi David Hartman, pioneer Israeli philosopher and modern Orthodox Rabbi, wrote in his book, *Conflicting Visions - Spiritual Possibilities for Israel* (Schocken, 1990), about the possibility for reconciliation between Israel and the Palestinians:

"Rosh Hashanah and Yom Kippur are...a corrective to the despair that pervades so many Jewish hearts today. The spirit of Rosh Hashanah and Yom Kippur should inspire Jews to proclaim clearly to the Palestinians that they are our brothers [and sisters] in creation, that we share a deep moral reverence for the sacredness of human life. Jews have come home to Israel because of their deep historical sense of community. However, in coming home, we do not seek to weaken or destroy our profound sense of brotherhood [and sisterhood] with the Palestinian people. It is imperative that our respective histories and traditions not destroy our common humanity born of our shared belief in God as Adonai of Creation and majestic moral [Ruler] of all humanity."

TO DISCUSS:

What has to happen before full peace can reign in the Middle East?

TO DO:

Today I will keep an open mind about reconciliation among the peoples of the Middle East.

20 Elul

TESHUVAH: ROOM FOR GROWTH

When Rabbi Mordecai M. Kaplan taught homiletics at the Jewish Theological Seminary, his practice was to explain the portion of the week on a Monday in a sermonic manner. On Wednesday, a senior student would present his version of the same biblical text. Dr. Kaplan was a very demanding and critical instructor, and the students dreaded the ordeal. Once in our class, a student took down verbatim what Dr. Kaplan said on Monday. When it came the student's turn to explain the passage on Wednesday, he repeated Kaplan's Monday interpretation word for word. At the end of the presentation, Dr. Kaplan said, "That's a terrible exposition." The student then complained, "But, Prof. Kaplan, that's exactly what you said Monday." And Kaplan replied, "Young man, I have grown since then."

Rabbi Bernard S. Raskas, *Heart of Wisdom*
(NY: United Synagogue - Burning Bush Press)

TO DISCUSS:

Is it possible to change one's mind so quickly? Was Rabbi Kaplan able to change his mind in a short space of time because of his great intellect? What other qualities are necessary for one to change one's mind?

TO DO:

Today I will think of old ideas of mine which need modification and adaptation.

21 Elul

IT IS NEVER TOO LATE

The last word has not been spoken,
the last sentence has not been written,
the final verdict is not in.
It is never too late
to change my mind,
my direction,
to say no to the past
and yes to the future,
to offer remorse,
to ask and give forgiveness.
It is never too late
to start over again,
to feel again
to love again
to hope again....

Rabbi Harold Schulweis

TO DISCUSS:

Is Rabbi Schulweis' poem too optimistic? Does it reflect a valid point of view about human nature?

TO DO:

Today I will say no to the past, and yes to the future. I will feel again, hope again, and love again.

22 Elul

TESHUVAH: TAKE CARE OF OTHERS

Rabbi Yisrael Salanter's student asked him a question: "How do you take care of your spiritual needs?"

He answered: "By taking care of the physical needs of others."

Setting out on a path of doing Teshuvah is easy from the perspective of Jewish tradition. A hasidic master once asked his students: How far is it from east to west? He answered: Easy - just one turn. Turn around in the opposite direction. The most important act of Teshuvah begins by turning around, taking one small step.

TO DISCUSS:

What is the meaning of Rabbi Salanter's answer? How else could he have answered?

TO DO:

Today I will care for some else's physical needs.

THE POWER OF OUR MOST BANAL ACTS

Not only do we fail to prepare for these days [of Awe] but we have far too limited an understanding of their potential. Our traditional conception of *teshuvah* is saying sorry to those we have wronged. We make our relationships with them whole again. We return a certain equilibrium to our community. But teshuvah can also be a transformational experience which makes us realize the impact of our most banal actions. Maimonides, the Rambam, describes the mental state we should adopt in approaching this process. We should think of ourselves and the world as perfectly balanced: exactly **half** guilty and **half** innocent. If we commit one sin we press down the scale of guilt against ourselves and the entire world and cause its destruction. And if we perform one good deed we press down the scale of merit and bring salvation to the entire world. Our simplest acts become infused with profound meaning.

Deborah E. Lipstadt, Dorot Professor of Modern Jewish and Holocaust Studies, Emory University, author of *Denying the Holocaust*. From *The Jewish Spectator*, Fall, 1993

TO DISCUSS:

What is the meaning of the expression, "God is in the details." How does that relate to Prof. Lipstadt's thoughts?

TO DO:

Today I will remember that every act of mine has the potential to save the world.

24 Elul

THE SOURCE OF TESHUVAH

Teshuvah is fundamentally a movement of return to originality, to the source of life and highest being in their wholeness

When we forget the essence of our soul itself, when we are distracted from introspection, from the content of inner life, everything becomes confused and doubtful. The beginning of repentance which immediately illumines the darkness is *that we return to ourselves, to the root of our soul, and we will at once return to God,* to the Soul of all Souls, and will strive even higher in holiness and purity. This is true for the individual and for the entire nation, for all of humanity, for the perfection of existence as a whole. Our ruin always comes when our soul *forgets itself.* And if ones claims there is a desire to return to God, but one does not summon itself to gather its exiles - *this repentance is a lie,* invoking God's name in vain. Only in the great truth of *return to oneself* will individuals and the nation repent, the world and all the worlds, all of being to their Maker, to the indwelling light of life. This is the secret of the Messiah's light, the appearance of the soul of the world, in whose brightness the world will return to the root of being, and the light of the Lord will shine upon him. And we will draw a life of holiness, of true *teshuvah,* from this great source of repentance.

Rav Avraham Yitzhak HaKohen Kook

TO DISCUSS:

How does Rav Kook define Teshuvah?

How is the return to self connected to the return to God?

TO DO:

Today I will begin to draw my inspiration for Teshuvah from the Source of all souls.

25 Elul

WE ARE BORN TO BE REFORMERS, RE-MAKERS

What is a man born for but to be a Reformer, a Re-maker of what man has made; a renouncer of lies; a restorer of truth and good, imitating that great Nature which embosoms us all, and which sleeps no moment on an old past, but every hour repairs herself, yielding us every morning a new day, and with every pulsation a new life? Let him renounce everything which is not true to him, and put all his practices back on their first thoughts, and do nothing for which he has not the whole world for his reason. If there are inconveniences, and what is called ruin in the way, because we have so enervated and maimed ourselves, yet it would be like dying of perfumes to sink in the effort to reattach the deeds of every day to the holy and mysterious recesses of life.

Ralph Waldo Emerson, "Man the Reformer"

TO DISCUSS:

How does restoring truth imitate Nature?

What is the interpretation of "doing nothing for which he has not the whole world for his reason"?

TO DO:

Today I will imitate Nature by restoring the good and the true, repairing myself every hour.

DON'T IGNORE THE CLOWNS

Soren Kierkegaard, the Danish theologian, often used stories as a vehicle to convey his message. He told of a circus coming to town, and of the circus people preparing for the show. One of the tents catches on fire. A clown, the only one of the circus people dressed, runs to the village asking the people to bring buckets of water to put out the fire. The townspeople, knowing that clowns are supposed to act that way, knowing that clowns are not serious, ignore the message until they see the smoke from the burning tent.

Throughout the year we live with the attitude of the villagers. We ignore the "clowns" of our day...the messengers of change...those who speak of wrong and injustice and hurt....

Like Gaul, so says a wit, morality is divided in three parts: right, wrong and everyone does it.... As you might guess, throughout the year we find "every one does it" as the odds on favor to describe our life style.

We live the words once spoken by Aldous Huxley, "The day will soon come when society will be controlled not by inflicting pain, but by inflicting pleasure." When the Berlin Wall came down, a bit of graffiti scrawled next to one of the holes in the wall stated, "I came, I saw, I did a little shopping."

Only "clowns" would decry a life style of pleasure. Only a fool would protest our finding life's lodestone "everyone is doing it," so I guess it's O.K......

During Elul the fire is seen. The clowns are heeded. We discover we all are clowns after all. We live with disguise and abandon. Now the fire is burning.

Selah lanu- forgive us, O God, for not listening to the cries of clowns!

Rabbi Samuel B. Press

TO DISCUSS:

Who are the "clowns," the messengers of change, whom we ignore today?

TO DO:

Today I will refuse to accept "Everyone is doing it" as my excuse for not changing my own ways.

27 Elul

WHERE GOD CAN'T ENTER

Wherever justice is perverted, there God is not. Wherever mercy is missing, there God is missing too.

I love the story about the poor man who tried to get into a rich "Schul," and they were too polite to say to him that they didn't want to let him in. So they put him off with one excuse after another. "You need letters of reference," and then, "You need to wait until the committee meets," and so on. Until finally, the poor man began to get the idea.

One day he went to the "Schul" and got rebuffed with the same excuse, and as he was walking away, feeling downhearted and depressed, he chanced to meet God. And God said, "Why do you look so sad?" The man said, "Because I've been trying to get into that "Schul" for months and I can't get in."

And God says, "I know how you feel. I've been trying to get into that "Schul" for years, and I can't get in either."

It makes no difference how fancy the furniture, or how many times God's name is invoked in a place. Either justice and mercy are there, or else God is not there either. That is the message of the period of the High Holy Days.

Rabbi Maurice Davis z"l

TO DISCUSS:

Do the synagogue you belong to, or the synagogue you attend, exhibit justice, mercy, and hospitality? How can you help to make your synagogue(s) more filled with these qualities?

TO DO:

Today I will begin to find ways to repair my synagogue to make it more of a place of warmth, hospitality, and equality.

28 Elul

COUNT YOUR CHANGE BEFORE LEAVING

Last week, I met someone I hadn't seen in several years, and after a big hello and exchange of greetings about family, friends, and health, the other person said to me: "You look great! You haven't changed a bit!"

After we parted, I thought about his statement that I haven't changed a bit. I suppose he meant that to be a compliment. He probably implied that since he last saw me, my hair was not any grayer, that I hadn't put on too much weight, and that I seemed to be in pretty good shape. I hadn't changed a bit! He meant it as a compliment and I took it as such.

During the period of the High Holidays, I wonder if "You haven't changed a bit" is a compliment. How does God see us today in comparison to last year? God would probably say to many of us: "You are in bad shape. You haven't changed a bit since last year."

In many stores, right near the cash register, there is a large sign which reads: "Count Your Change Before Leaving." I think this reminder applies not only to cash. **Count your change** is very good spiritual advice as well. Each of us should be able to list and count the ways in which we have changed for the better since last Yom Kippur.

As we approach the new Hebrew year, let us count our change on a regular basis. Let us make sure that when God sees us, we will hear, "You look great! You've changed a lot

56

since last year." Then we can look forward to a new year marked by further growth and greater understanding, a year in which we will be deserving of God's blessings of contentment, good heath, and nachas for ourselves and our families.

Rabbi Joseph Braver z"l

TO DISCUSS:

How have you changed since last Yom Kippur? How would you like to change during the coming year?

TO DO:

Today I will endeavor the think of personal change as a positive direction in my life.

Today I will seek new ways to change my life for the better.

29 Elul

HINENI - HERE I AM!

On Rosh Hashanah, the Torah reading speaks of God's call to Avraham. Avraham's response is <u>Hineni</u>. "Here I am." That call is sent forth to every person in every generation, a challenge and an awakening. The following poem will help us to reflect on the spirit of the High Holy Days. I hope that we will learn to respond in the affirmative, as Avraham did.

<u>Hineni</u>
<u>Hineni</u>. Here I am.
A little bit nervous, a little bit self conscious.
After all, whom am I talking to?
And what have I done?
Am I a sinner in search of grace
or a saint seeking salvation?
Am I so evil
or so good
as to warrant this season of introspection?
And yet here it is, and here I am:
this time of change and correction.
this heart of confusion and contrition.
Oh, if I could change!
If I could be so sure of myself
that I no longer had to imagine the sights of others;
to be so loving of myself
that I no longer had to ration my loving of others;

to be so bold with myself
that I no longer had to fear the bravery of others.
Oh, if I could change
there is so much I would change.
Maybe I will, but it scares me so.
Maybe I won't and that should scare me more,
But it doesn't.
So let me pray just this:
Let no one be put to shame because of me.
Wouldn't that make this a wonderful year?
Hineni. Here I am

Rabbi Rami Shapiro

TO DISCUSS:

What obstacles are there in the way of people's ability to change?

What obstacles in your life would you like to begin to work on to facilitate your own positive change?

TO DO:

Today I will overcome some of my fear of change.

From Elul To Tishre

"I AM CANCELLING MY WORD AND FULFILLING YOURS" THE THIRTEEN DIVINE ATTRIBUTES

The version of the Thirteen Divine Attributes (Shlosh Esray Midot) in the Mahzor is radically different from the biblical version. The rabbis cut the verse in half when quoting it in the High Holiday liturgy, and reverse its meaning. In the Torah it states that God will punish the children for the sins of their parents. Obviously feeling uncomfortable with this outdated theology , the rabbis cut off the biblical verse just before the word "no," when it says that God will not forgive the next generation.

The following Midrash clarifies why the rabbis chose to do this, and justify it by putting the change in the mouth of God:

When the Blessed Holy One said to Moshe:

"...visiting the iniquity of the parents upon the children"
(Exodus 20:5).

Moshe said:

Many are the wicked who have begotten righteous children;

shall they take the consequences of their parents' iniquities?

Terah served images, and Avraham, his son, was righteous,

the same with Hezekiah who was righteous, and Ahaz his father wicked;

the same with Josiah who was righteous, and Amon his

father wicked.

Is it right then that the righteous be struck down for the iniquity of the parents?

The Blessed Holy One, said:

By your life, I am voiding my words and fulfilling yours.

As it is said: "Parents shall not be put to death for children, nor children for parents" (Deut. 24:16).

And, by your life, I am writing them down in your name, as it is said: "According to that which is written in the book of the Torah of Moshe" (II Kings 14:6).

Midrash - *Leviticus Rabbah* 19:20

TO DISCUSS:

Were the rabbis justified in re-interpreting a biblical verse?

Why are God's Thirteen Attributes quoted so often in the Mahzor?

TO DO:

As I approach the Days of Awe, I will place God's qualities of mercy in my mind at all times.

1 Tishre - ROSH HASHANAH

TESHUVAH: MUCH MORE THAN
REPENTANCE

Every major author, from the medieval sage
Maimonides, to modern philosophers and theologians,
attests to the fact that Teshuvah is not just "repentance."
The Rambam, in his classic work, the Mishneh Torah,
urges his readers to reach out to people who were harmed,
and that the power of confession is enormous in healing
old wounds. The modern saint, and some say Maimonides'
20th century counterpart, Adin Steinsaltz, in his book
Teshuvah, takes the position that teshuvah is a spiritual
awakening, a desire to strengthen the bond between us and
the holy in all Being.

Rabbi Pinchas Peli, in his book outlining Rav
Soloveitchik's ideas on Teshuvah, explains that it connotes
not just remorse, but a complete break from the old
environment and the old self - the veritable creation of a
new personality.

Clearly, the idea of teshuvah is one of the most cogent
theological concepts ever created by any tradition, ancient
or modern, in empowering human beings to make new
beginnings and to re-create their own lives.

Rabbi Dov Peretz Elkins

TO DISCUSS:

How has Jewish tradition expanded and enhanced the rabbinic idea of Teshuvah?

TO DO:

Today, the first day of the new Jewish year, I will strive for spiritual awakening, and the recreation of my whole being.

2 Tishre - ROSH HASHANAH

Hayom Harat Olam - Today Is The Birthday of The World

WHY NOT YOU?

On this Rosh Hashanah, this second chance for change, this birthday of a new year and a new you, I ask, "Why not you?" Why not you, watching the morning mist rise over the mountains of Scotland? Why not you catching a play on the London stage, standing on top of the Eiffel Tower, or gazing directly at the Mona Lisa in Paris? Why not you, walking the Great Wall in China, riding the Bullet Train in Japan, visiting the out-back of Australia to catch a glimpse of a kangaroo? Why not you, sailing the lands of Venice on a gondola with someone you love, catching a sunrise from the top of Masada and gazing down at the austere beauty of the Dead Sea?

And why not you, embracing the Jewish idea of **Tikkun Olam**, taking part in the life task of making whole the broken fragments of the world? Why not you, inventing a new product, creating a new idea, changing someone's life or inspiring another through your own inspiration? Why not you, being happy, joyful, filling your life with loving, giving, sharing, caring, touching, laughter and tenderness? Why not you, wealthy, successful, satisfied, productive, creative, enthusiastic, courageous, energetic, purposeful?

Rabbi Steven Carr Reuben

TO DISCUSS:

Which of the ideas suggested by Rabbi Reuben are possible for you to try in the coming year?

Which would give you the most fulfillment?

What, other than finances, has been holding you back?

TO DO:

Today, in the year that begins now, I will ask myself: "Why not me?" and begin to fulfill an important dream for my life.

3 Tishre

MAKING A DIFFERENCE - ONE BY ONE

As the old man walked the beach at dawn, he noticed a young man ahead of him picking up starfish and flinging them into the sea. Finally catching up with the youth, he asked him why he was doing this. The answer was that the stranded starfish would die if left until the morning sun.

"But the beach goes on for miles and there are millions of starfish," countered the other. "How can your effort make any difference?"

The young man looked at the starfish in his hand and then threw it to safety in the waves. "It makes a difference to this one."

TO DISCUSS:

When have you felt frustrated that your small contribution can hardly make a difference in the grand scheme of things?

How did you resolve your dilemma?

TO DO:

Today I will take some small steps to clean up and repair my tiny corner of the world.

4 Tishre

CAN YOU CROSS THE RIVER?

Rabbi Pinhas ben Yair was going to the House of Study, but the river Ginnai was too strong for him.

He said to it:

Ginnai, Ginnai, why do you keep me from the House of Study?

It parted before him, and he passed.

His disciples said to him: Could we pass too?

He said to them:

One who knows in the heart that he/she has never injured any human being can pass without harm.

Talmud Yerushalmi, Demai 22A (adapted from *Hammer On The Rock*, ed. Nahum N. Glatzer p. 37)

TO DISCUSS:

What is the point of the story?

What lessons does it have for us during the Days of Awe?

TO DO:

During these Ten Days of Teshuvah, and after, I resolve to try not to hurt any human being.

During these Ten Days of Teshuvah, and after, I resolve to respect every creature as made in the image of God.

5 Tishre

FOUR RESULTS OF SIN

What happens to the sinner according to Jewish Tradition? Since Judaism never has just one answer to a question, the Midrash supplies for possibilities, according to which biblical book one consults. Four different verses are quoted in one Midrash, each with its own theological approach. The biblical books in this Midrash are personified.

1) Wisdom was asked: The sinner, what is his destiny?
She said to those who asked: "Evil pursues sinners" (Proverbs 13:21).

2) Prophecy was asked: The sinner, what is her destiny?
She said to those who asked: "The soul that sins, it shall die" (Ezekiel 18:4).

3) The Torah was asked: The sinner, what is his destiny?
She said to those who asked: "Let her bring a guilt-offering,
and atonement for her" (Leviticus 1:4)

4) The Blessed Holy One was asked:
The sinner, what is his destiny?
God said to those who asked:

Let them turn in repentance, and atonement
   shall be made for them;
as it is written:
"Good and upright is the Lord; therefore God
   instructs sinners in the way" (Psalm 25:8)

Midrash - *Psekita De-Rav Kahana* 158A

TO DISCUSS:

Explain the four answers given by the Midrash.

How does God's answer differ from the others?

Comment on the ability of the Midrash to go beyond the
letter of the Bible.

TO DO:

Today I will look to God to help me and others find ways
to improve our deeds, and to transcend our past.

6 Tishre

THE SOUND OF THE SHOFAR

May the sound of the <u>shofar</u> shatter our complacency
And make us conscious of the corruptions in our lives.
May the sound of the <u>shofar</u> penetrate our souls,
And cause us to turn to our Father in Heaven.
May the sound of the <u>shofar</u> break the bonds of our enslavement to the evil impulse.
And enable us to serve God with a whole heart.
May the sound of the <u>shofar</u> renew our loyalty to the one true King
And strengthen our determination to defy the false gods.
May the sound of the <u>shofar</u> awaken us to the enormity of our sins
And the vastness of God's mercy for those who truly repent.
May the sound of the <u>shofar</u> summon us to service
And stir us to respond, as did Abraham, "Here am I."
May the sound of the <u>shofar</u> recall the moment
When we stood at Mount Sinai and uttered the promise:
"All that God has spoken, we will do and obey."
May the sound of the <u>shofar</u> recall the promise

of the ingathering of the exiles,
And stir within us renewed devotion to the
land of Israel.
May the sound of the shofar recall the vision
of the prophets,
Of the day when all people will live in peace.
May the sound of the shofar awaken us to the
flight of time,
And summon us to spend our days with
purpose.
May the sound of the shofar remind us that it
is time to
"Proclaim liberty throughout the land
To all the inhabitants thereof."
May the sound of the shofar become our
jubilant shout of joy.
On the day of the promised, long-awaited
redemption.
May the sound of the shofar enter our hearts:
For blessed is the people that hearkens to its
call.
Rabbi Hershel Matt, *Walking Humbly With God*
(KTAV, 1993)

TO DISCUSS:
Which meanings of the Shofar resonate most powerfully
for you?

TO DO:
Today I will let the sound of the Shofar awaken me to the
flight of time, and summon me to spend my days with
purpose.

73

7 Tishre

NO SAINT IS WITHOUT SIN

It is curious and paradoxical that *Teshuvah* is numbered among the 613 mitzvot set down according to tradition by the Torah. Repentance, as Teshuvah is commonly rendered, is thus the obligation even of one who fulfills with exemplary devotion and in scrupulous detail the other 612 Biblical prescriptions. Teshuvah speaks to all of us—to the respectable and righteous as well as to the "enemy of society," the outcast, the criminal, the renegade—and it speaks in all seasons.

Teshuvah is always available to us. Because we are sin-prone, our fallibility and frailty expose us to temptation and error, and we can never relax in the assurance that our virtue is so fully and definitely rooted that it cannot be dislodged. Indeed, this very sense of the security of our righteousness may itself be the thrust of the sin of haughtiness. With virtue as with humility, self-consciousness is fatal. Albert Schweitzer once remarked, "A good conscience is the invention of the devil."

Teshuvah, as Judaism understands it, indicates that we may never lay down our arms in our struggle with sin. The price of righteousness, like that of liberty, is eternal vigilance. The records contain many instances of people who through the years gained a deserved reputation for honor and integrity, and indeed were held up as exemplars of the good life, but who succumbed to an overwhelming temptation, reflecting a weariness that they had never before betrayed. In an instant of surrender they destroyed that which had taken a lifetime to establish.

Adapted from Rabbi Morris Adler, *May I Have A Word With You?* NY: Crown Publishers

TO DISCUSS:

Why are even the most pious subject to the dangers of the *Yetzer Ha-Ra* (the evil impulse)?

What remedy is there?

TO DO:

I resolve to be eternally vigilant in preserving my clear conscience.

8 Tishre

CHANGE BEGINS WITH ME

Vice-President Al Gore tells, in his book, *Earth In The Balance* (Houghton Mifflin, 1992, p. 14) why he thinks that change must begin inside a person's heart.

He tells the story of Mahatma Gandhi who said: "We must be the change we wish to see in the world." Gandhi was approached by a woman who was very concerned that her son consumed too much sugar, and was worried about his health. She asked Gandhi to tell the child about the harmful effects of sugar in the hope that he would listen and cease eating it.

Gandhi was happy to assist, but asked the woman to return with her son in two weeks, not before.

Two weeks passed and the woman and her son came to Gandhi. The sage spoke with the boy, and recommended that he stop eating sugar. The boy agreed, and the mother was extremely grateful.

"But why," she asked, "did you insist on the two week period of waiting?"

"Because," replied Ghandi, "I needed the two weeks to stop eating sugar myself."

TO DISCUSS:

Think of examples of people who try to encourage others to change, when they themselves do not. For example, doctors who lead unhealthy life styles. What other examples can you give?

TO DO:

Today I will set an example of change and only then suggest that others follow my example.

9 Tishre

On this eve of Yom Kippur, the most sacred day in the Jewish calendar, we prepare ourselves for a lengthened period of prayer, thought, repentance and self-reflection.

Much of what we say during this evening's prayers and tomorrow's liturgy will be what we have been saying and doing since Rosh Hashanah and before, during Elul.

We know that much of our repentance will be for things which have been ingrained in us for many years, and which we have tried to change in the past, without great success.

Nevertheless we plug ahead, persist, recite the same prayers, ask for the same forgiveness, and do not give up hope that maybe this time it will work better than it did last year.

Once a pious person in a religious order was asked what it is that the residents do inside the walls of the community. He answered: "We fall and get up, fall and get up, fall and get up again."

Rabbi Dov Peretz Elkins

TO DISCUSS:

Do you believe that human nature can change?

Shall we persist in our rituals of atonement, if in all probability we may repeat some of the same mistakes again?

TO DO:

The high ideals of Teshuvah deserve my best efforts. If I fail, I will try again. And again. And again.

10 Tishre - Yom Kippur

LESSONS FROM A FISH

In a recent article in the New York Times it was reported that scientists discovered a fish that changes shape when it detects the presence of hungry predators. It transforms itself from something that is easily swallowed into something difficult to swallow.

What an amazing feat!

The researchers commented on their discovery:

"Plasticity is the only way for an organism to adapt to a rapidly changing environment within its life span.... This opens up the door for more careful examination of plasticity in vertebrates. People are going to have to stop thinking that there's not going to be this kind of change during an individual's lifetime."

This particular fish changes in order to survive. We humans need to learn that in order to survive we too need to learn the trick of changing our shape, our attitude, our values, and our actions. In order to survive as moral, value-oriented creatures, we often need to make large and small changes in our personalities, our souls, our selves.

Change, in short, or Teshuvah, as our ancestors called it, is the key to survival, in an ever increasingly changing world.

Rabbi Dov Peretz Elkins

TO DISCUSS:

Did God create fish to change in order to provide an example for higher level creatures?

TO DO:

On this sacred Day of Atonement, I will try harder than ever to be "At One" with my self and my God.

I will recognize God's plan for all creatures to change in order to survive.

ABOUT THE EDITOR

Dov Peretz Elkins, spiritual leader of Princeton's Jewish Center, is well-known as a prominent Rabbi and innovative Jewish educator. Rabbi Elkins has been a pioneer in interactive, affective and humanistic learning models for twenty-five years. His was one of the first Jewish educators to promote family education in Jewish schools and in synagogue and other Jewish communal settings. Trained in Human Resource Development by University Associates, The Gestalt Institute, NTL Institute, and many other prominent growth and learning centers around North America, his 25 pioneering books can be found on the shelf of every Jewish communal service worker, educator and rabbi.

At age 21 Elkins received the coveted and prestigious recognition from the Hebrew University of Jerusalem by receiving the "Amit Yerushalayim" certificate for proficiency in Hebrew language.

Commenting on Elkins' first book, *Worlds Lost and Found: Discoveries in Biblical Archeology* (Abelard-Schuman, 1964), co-authored with the century's leading Jewish educator, Azriel Eisenberg, Prime Minister David Ben-Gurion of Israel wrote: "This is one of the most interesting books ever published on the ancient world." *Worlds Lost and Found* received the Jewish Book Council Award.

Rabbi Elkins' ordination is from the Jewish Theological Seminary, and his doctorate in pastoral counseling and family education from Colgate Rochester Divinity School. In 1990 he received the honorary Doctor of Divinity degree from his alma mater, JTS, and in 1995 he received the Distinguished Alumni Award from Gratz College, Philadelphia.

Dr. Elkins has earned the respect and admiration of colleagues and students throughout the world for his many previous works on self-esteem, experiential learning and spiritual renewal. He has lectured and conducted training workshops throughout North America, Europe, Russia, Africa and Israel. His lectures and writings have earned him a reputation as a youthful, dynamic and passionate innovator and trail-blazing spiritual leader.

Dov Peretz Elkins' writings, a unique blend of religion, education, psychology and spirituality, mixed with a deep commitment to social change and human betterment, have earned him a reputation of a leading change agent and religious spokesperson of our day.

Rabbi Elkins lives in Princeton, NJ, with his wife Maxine. Their six children live in Los Angeles, Tel Aviv, Jerusalem, Philadelphia and Pittsburgh.

"No Rabbi should be without it. *Moments* makes the Mahzor more contemporary than anything I have ever seen."
Rabbi Stephen Chaim Listfield

"Dov Elkins' annual *Moments of Transcendence* Supplement helps enrich the spiritual experience for both rabbi and congregation. I can't imagine the High Holidays without it."
Rabbi Ira Korinow

"I use Dov's wonderful readings, poems, motivating selections to enrich and enliven my High Holidays every year, and wouldn't do without it."
Rabbi Kenneth L. Cohen

"The books and annual supplements are called *Moments of Transcendence*, but they provide hours and hours of thought-provoking ideas that save days and days of effort in preparing for the High Holidays."
Rabbi Mitchell Wohlberg, Baltimore

"There is so much here for engaging the heart, inspiring thought and elevating the spirit! An enriching and valuable aid to any rabbi."
Rabbi Jacob S. Rubenstein, President, Rabbinical Council of America, Rabbi, Young Israel of Scarsdale

"The material in *Moments* is replete with thoughtful insights that are of immeasurable help to the Rabbi, who, under great pressure, must come up with interesting material for these important days."
Rabbi Reuven Bulka, Ottawa

"Very useful, informative and inspiring."
Rabbi Benzion Kaganoff, Chicago

"An invaluable aid for the contemporary Jewish preacher."
Rabbi Abner Weiss, Los Angeles

"Rabbi Elkins' work will surely contribute to elevating the spirituality of any High Holiday Service."
Rabbi Doniel Kramer, National Director, UJA Rabbinic Cabinet

"For anyone looking for supplementary materials to embellish high holiday services, I encourage you to get copies of Dov Peretz Elkins' *Moments of Transcendence*, both the original volumes, and subsequent expansions of the core collection. There are some truly excellent items, organized in an easily accessible manner. It's really a treasure, and, used judiciously, can provide materials for years to come."
Rabbi Larry Pinsker

"Let me say to you-the stuff keeps my HH explanations fresh every year. The collections are nothing short of excellent."
Rabbi Andrew Sacks, Israel Director, The Rabbinical Assembly

"Dov Peretz Elkins' *Moments of Transcendence* is particularly good and useful...and this endorsement comes from someone who also turns out these things, so it must be sincere."
Rabbi Jack Riemer

Growth Associates

Human Relations Consultants & Publishers
212 Stuart Road East   Princeton, NJ 08540-1946
609/497-7375   E-mail: elkins@tigger.jvnc.net   Web Site: www.DPElkins.com

ORDER FORM
Please Print or Type

NAME: _____ DATE: _____

ADDRESS: _____

CITY, STATE, ZIP: _____

TELEPHONE: _____ E-mail: _____

Educational Materials by Dr. Dov Peretz Elkins

Qty	Titles Available	Cost	Total
	Moments of Transcendence: Devotional Commentson the High		
	Holy Mahzor		
	1992 Supplement	$20	
	1993 Supplement	$20	
	1994-5 Supplement	$40	
	1996 Supplement	$20	
	1997 Supplement	$20	
	1998 Supplement (enlarged)	$30	
	NEW 1999 Supplement (enlarged)	$30	
	2-Volume Hardcover Edition (Jason Aronson, 1992)		
	Vol 1: Rosh Hashanah, Vol 2: Yom Kippur ($40 each)	$80	
	NEW *Forty Days of Transformation: Daily Reflections of Teshuvah*		
	for Spiritual Growth from Rosh Hodesh Elul to Yom Kippur		
	(Quantity Discount)	$15	
	NEW *Meditations for the Days of Awe: Reflections, Guided Imagery*		
	& Other Creative Exercises To Enrich Your Spiritual Life	$20	
	NEW *A Shabat Reader: the Universe of Cosmic Joy*		
	(anthology of 40 selections including Ismar Schorsch, Arthur		
	Green, Blu Greenberg, Lawrence Kushner, Harold Schulweis,		
	Gunther Plaut, Michael Lerner, Gershom Scholem, Amy		
	Eilberg, Sue Levi Elwell)	$14	
	NEW *For Israel's 50th Anniversary and Beyond:A Treasury of*	$50	
	Israel and Zionism: A Sourcebook for Speakers, Writers and		
	Teachers. (Loose Leaf with 40 tabbed chapters) Computer disk		
	available only with book. (Disk contains file for each chapter).	Disk	
	(ed. D. P. Elkins & J. Kalmanofsky)	$25	
	Hasidic Wisdom: Sayings From the Jewish Sages by Simcha Raz, trans.	$35	
	Dov Peretz Elkins and Jonathan Elkins. Best collection		
	available of Hasidic aphorisms; Hebrew edition (Pitgamay		
	Hasidim) best-seller in Israel since 1981.		

Jewish Guided Imagery: A How-To Book For Rabbis, Educators, & group Leaders (for accompanying cassette audiotape with imagery scripts, add $10)	$35 Tape $10
Melodies From My Father's House: Hasidic Wisdom for the Heart & Soul ed. Simcha Raz. Selected & trans. Dov Peretz Elkins, calligraphy and artwork by Michele Demak Epstein.	$12
Four Questions On the Sidrah - Sheet for each Sidrah Format arranged to be copied and distributed to congregations and schools. (Similar to Sidrah Sparks)	$45
Sidrah Sparks - Weekly Torah Lessons & Questions for Discussion Double-sided sheet for each weekly Parashah - Format arranged to be copied & distributed to members of congregations and schools. Used by synagogues, day & supplementary schools throughout North America. (Similar to Four Questions On the Sidrah)	$45
NEW *More Sidrah Sparks* - Another volume in above series-1999	$45
Shepherd of Jerusalem - A Biography of Rabbi Abraham Isaac Kook (Jason Aronson, 1995)	$20
Prescription For a Long & Happy Life - Age-Old Wisdom For the New Age Hardcover - Sermons & Essays	$20
Humanizing Jewish Life: Judaism and the Human Potential Movement	$12
My Seventy-Two Friends: Encounters With Refuseniks in the USSR	$12
Organizational Development for Jewish Groups: Theory, Practice, & Exercises.	$8
Experimental Programs for Jewish Groups: 30 Full-Length Programs	$10
Clarifying Jewish Values: 25 Values Activities for Jewish Groups	$10
Jewish Consciousness Raising: 50 Experimental Exercises	$10
Loving My Jewishness: Jewish Self-Pride and Self-Esteem. A text for adult & teenage groups. Ten or more copies @ $5, including Leader's Guide.	$10
Teaching People to Love Themselves: A Leader's Handbook of Theory & Technique for Self-Esteem training. Includes 50 experiential exercises. *BEST SELLER*	$22
Glad to Be Me: Building Self-Esteem in Yourself & Others, Collection of readings and photos-revised and expaned edition *BEST SELLER*	$12
Twelve Pathways to Feeling Better About Yourself	$7.50
Self- Concept Source Book: Ideas & Activities for Building Self-Esteem	$19
The Ideal Jew: Values Clarification Program (Leader's guide & 15 cc.)	Set $10
Why Did Susan Cohen Desert Judaism? Values Clarification Program on Intermarriage, Assimilation (Leader's guide & 15 cc.)	Set $10
God's Warriors: Dramatic Adventures of Rabbis in Uniform	$10
Rejoice With Jerusalem: Prayers, Readings, & Songs for Israel Observances	$6
The Tallit: Some Modern Meanings (Jewish Tract Series)	$3

All orders must be prepaid in U.S. Funds only.   Subtotal: _____
Shipping & Handling: 15% of order; (10% of order over $150)   S&H: _____
     Orders from Canada: 20% of order; other foreign orders: 30% of order
Make checks payable to Dov Peretz Elkins, **minimum order: $3.**   Total: _____
_____ Check here if interested in inviting Dr. Elkins to give lectures,
workshops, retreats, and/or other training events for board, staff or faculty, etc.